BOOTCAMP
8 BOOKS TO
REWRITE MINDSETS

INTO WINNING STATES OF MIND

by LINKEDIN AND TOWN HALL ACHIEVER OF THE YEAR
EY NOMINEE ENTREPRENEUR OF THE YEAR
GRAND HOMAGE LYS DIVERSITY

Dr BAK NGUYEN, DMD

TO ALL THOSE LOOKING TO BE MORE, TO HAVE MORE, TO
BREAK THE BOUNDARIES IN 8 WEEKS.

by Dr BAK NGUYEN

ISBN: 978-1-989536-46-9

ABOUT THE AUTHOR

From Canada, **Dr BAK NGUYEN**, Nominee EY Entrepreneur of the year, Grand Homage LYS DIVERSITY, and LinkedIn & TownHall Achiever of the year. Dr Bak is a cosmetic dentist, CEO and founder of Mdex & Co. His company is revolutionizing the dental field. Speaker and motivator, he wrote more than 70 books in 35 months accumulating many world records (to be officialized). He is on the quest to set the next word record of writing 72 books / 36 months. His books are covering:

- **ENTREPRENEURSHIP**
- **LEADERSHIP**
- **QUEST OF IDENTITY**
- **DENTISTRY AND MEDICINE**
- **PARENTING**
- **CHILDREN BOOKS**
- **PHILOSOPHY**

In 2003, he founded Mdex, a dental company upon which in 2018, he launched the most ambitious private endeavour to reform the dental industry, Canada wide. Philosopher, he has close to his heart the quest of happiness of the people surrounding him, patients and colleagues alike. In 2020, he launched an International collaborative initiative named **THE ALPHAS** to share knowledge and to Entrepreneurs and Doctors to thrive through the Greatest Pandemic and Economic depression of our time.

These projects have allowed Dr Nguyen to attract interests from the international and diplomatic community and he is now the center of a global discussion in the wellbeing and the future of the health profession. It is in that matter that he shares his thoughts and encourages the health community to share their own stories.

"It's not worth it go through it alone! Together, we stand, alone, we fall."

Motivational speaker and serial entrepreneur, philosopher and author, from his own words, Dr Nguyen describes himself as a dentist by circumstances, an entrepreneur by nature and a communicator by passion.

He also holds recognitions from the Canadian Parliament and the Canadian Senate.

BOOTCAMP

8 BOOKS TO

REWRITE MINDSETS

INTO WINNING STATES OF MIND

by Dr BAK NGUYEN

INTRODUCTION

BY Dr BAK NGUYEN

THE ALCHEMIST
by Paulo Coelho
CHAPTER 1 - Dr BAK NGUYEN

RICH DAD POOR DAD
by Robert Kiyosaki and Sharon Lechter
CHAPTER 2 - Dr BAK NGUYEN

THE COMPOUND EFFECT
by Darren Hardy
CHAPTER 3 - Dr BAK NGUYEN

THIS IS YOUR TIME
by Joel Osteen
CHAPTER 4 - Dr BAK NGUYEN

PART II

THE SECOND COMING OF STEVE JOBS
by Alan Deutschman
CHAPTER 5 - Dr BAK NGUYEN

BUSINESS @ THE SPEED OF THOUGHT
by Bill Gates and Collins Hemingway
CHAPTER 6 - Dr BAK NGUYEN

DELIVERING HAPPINESS
by Tony Hsieh
CHAPTER 7 - Dr BAK NGUYEN

WIKINOMICS: HOW MASS COLLABORATION CHANGES EVERYTHING
by Don Tapscott and Anthony D. Williams
CHAPTER 8 - Dr BAK NGUYEN

CONCLUSION

BY Dr BAK NGUYEN

INTRODUCTION

by Dr BAK NGUYEN

I am speechless. Speechless because Life happens as you start to say YES! The month of August is starting, and I am ahead, writing a book every 8 days for 8 straight weeks. This is my 71st book. Keeping my current pace, I might be done before the end of this month.

Not all the books took 8 days, **EMPOWERMENT** was written within 31 hours. All of this to set the next world record of writing 72 books over a period of 36 months. But that's not the reason why I am speechless.

On a journey to empower womankind, I just finished writing my 70th book, **THE MODERN WOMAN, TO HAVE IT ALL WITHOUT SACRIFICE** with Dr Emily Letran. As I wasn't sure where it would lead, I took a chance. Emily is a fantastic person, full of energy and positivity. She also has her ways to get things done. She, herself had already written 4 published books.

It all started on an interview on the **ALPHASHOW**. We were killing it, having much fun sharing the screen. After the interview, I proposed to her to co-write a book together. And this is how it all started. I learned to work with Emily, who is a force of nature, I grew much from the experience.

Emily then introduced me to Sharon Lechter, our special guest author, her mentor. I am very open to meet and to greet new people into my life. I did not know who Sharon Lechter was, until Emily mentioned **RICH DAD POOR DAD**! That book rewrote my **DNA** and turned my mindset 180 degrees. Well, Sharon Lechter is the co-author of that book.

I hid my emotions not to be impressed. Wasn't it Robert Kiyosaki who wrote the book? I read the book in print but also bought the audiobooks narrated by Robert himself. That's how I learned about Robert Kiyosaki, from his voice going through all of his books, the whole collection.

As I arrived at Sharon Lechter's chapter, I read it. I was trembling of emotions as I relived through her words and style my feelings as I was looking for myself. I had a moment, frozen in time.

They say never to meet your idols. Well, I did better, I wrote with one of mind. I can never thank Emily enough for her kindness and generosity to have introduced Sharon to me. From the bottom of my heart, thank you Dr Letran.

As I was looking for the next book to write, I couldn't escape the souvenir and the imagery from the past. Usually, I try not to open that door, looking back. The last time I did, after receiving the **LINKEDIN AWARD AND TOWNHALL** as **ACHIEVER OF THE YEAR**, I got vertigo as I was looking back.

Strange thing, but looking back, even at my success, wasn't a good feeling. It took me the whole weekend to reestablish balance, looking forward. But this time, it is different. The feeling is one of joy, like looking back on a childhood memory. Not too long ago, I was such a different person.

To write about the books that made me into what I am today was a crazy idea that crossed my mind for a minute. Then, I rejected the idea since I have so much more subjects to cover and I am not a YOU TUBER reviewing lens and cameras.

It is then that I met with Leo, my newest protege. He was introduced to me by my friend and brother, strategist Jonas Diop. I spent an hour with Leo, out of respect for Jonas.

Leo is 19-year-old and very polite. What stroke me as special is that he successfully kept me engaged in the conversation in interesting matters for more than an hour, taking about mindsets and success.

Leo was drinking my words, one after the next, to figure out how to propel himself forward. Looking at him, I try to put myself in his shoes to know what it feels like to listen to Dr Bak… I know, it may sound narcissistic, but really, I have no clue of my impact on people. Leo became my mirror for the duration of a conversation.

The feeling I had was the same one as the moment I realized that I was writing with someone who rewrote my mindset 15 years ago.

In the **MODERN WOMAN**, one of my last chapters was about **MENTORS**. Within my last books, I took the habit to talk about my mentors and to thank them for their influence on me.

"To me, gratitude is a way to
look back without vertigo."
Dr Bak Nguyen

As I didn't know who Sharon Lechter really was before reading her chapter as a guest author, I realized that I had many more mentors, mentors that I haven't met in real life but who has influenced and changed the course of my life in ways that I can even begin to explain.

This is why I am writing this book, **BOOTCAMP**, dedicated to the mentors and teachers I had in my life, mentors I met in books and audiobooks. Then, I started to write down the titles that changed my life.

Before I started writing, I read so many books, mostly audiobooks. For as long as it was about finance, personal growth and strategy, name it, I read it. Usually, I listen to these audiobooks while driving from one city to the next. Toronto, New York, Boston,

Ottawa, Detroit, I learned so much on the road to these metropolis.

That is the main reason why I tend to avoid the classrooms and the seminars. I am learning so much more listening to audiobooks on the way to those events. The event gave me an excuse to learn, but not in the classroom. That being said, I never had the chance to honor these great minds who shaped mine.

Just like Leo, I look up to so many great people, and they may want the feedback of gratitude, that exact feedback that I am actively looking for to keep moving forward. I wrote 70 books within 35 months. Many years before I wrote my first words, well, I read their words and thoughts.

Well, this book, **BOOTCAMP: 8 BOOKS TO REWRITE MINDSETS INTO WINNING STATES OF MIND** is the first volume to honor my mentors, those I haven't met yet. I chose 8 books because each can be read within a week. So 8 books, 8 weeks, this is a Bootcamp that will reshape any mind into one that will win, scoring daily. And 8 is also the number of the Dragon, infinity.

Even better, going through a Bootcamp, it is not only the thinking that will shift (your mindset) but you will experience the sensation to be lifted up from your current state, to feel the power to follow your dreams and to change the world. That's the state of mind that will change the present course of your destiny.

This will be a hell of a ride, one that will change your life forever! Out of respect for my mentors, I will not summarize their books. There is no shortcut, you will have to read their books. But, what I will do is to take one passage that I can remember clearly without note and without looking back at that book, and tell you how it changed my mindset.

I will introduce you to my mentors and tell you my story. For you to start your Bootcamp, you will have to sign up with each of them, opening up their books.

And sure, I am looking to finally meet with them, to have a chance to thank them for how they changed my life, just like I might have the opportunity to thank Sharon Lechter in person. And one day perhaps, you and I might meet in person too. This isn't about pride and fame, but gratitude and connection.

In the meantime, are you ready to change? Your Bootcamp starts now.

From **MILLION DOLLAR MINDSET,** this is **BOOTCAMP: 8 BOOKS TO REWRITE MINDSETS INTO WINNING STATES OF MIND.** Welcome to the **ALPHAS**.

Dr BAK NGUYEN

CHAPTER 1
"THE ALCHEMIST
FROM PAULO COELHO"
by Dr BAK NGUYEN

PAULO COELHO, multiple times awarded Brazilian Author of 32 books between 1974 and 2018. This list of his awards and honors goes on for pages 1995 and 2008. His book, The Alchemist, made him famous. He's sold 35 million copies.

HANS CHRISTIAN ANDERSEN AWARD, DENMARK, 2007 - ASSOCIATION OF MEXICAN BOOKSELLERS LAS PERGOLAS PRIZE, MEXICO, 2006 - I PREMIO ÁLAVA EN EL CORAZÓN PRIZE, SPAIN - 2006 CRUZ DO MÉRITO DO EMPREENDEDOR JUSCELINO KUBITSCHEK, BRAZIL - 2006 THE RELIGION COMMUNICATORS COUNCIL WILBUR AWARD, U.S., 2006 - THE ZAHIR—KIKLOP LITERARY AWARD HIT OF THE YEAR, CROATIA, 2006 - DIRECTGROUP INTERNATIONAL AUTHOR AWARD, GERMANY, 2005 - GOLDENE FEDER AWARD, GERMANY, 2005 - BUDAPEST INTERNATIONAL BOOK FESTIVAL BUDAPEST PRIZE, HUNGARY, 2005 - ORDER OF HONOUR OF UKRAINE, UKRAINE, 2004 - ORDER OF ST. SOPHIA FOR CONTRIBUTION TO REVIVAL OF SCIENCE AND CULTURE, UKRAINE, 2004 - THE ALCHEMIST—NIELSEN GOLD BOOK AWARD, UK, 2004 - ELEVEN MINUTES—EX LIBRIS AWARD, SERBIA, 2004

VEČERNJE NOVOSTI NEWSPAPER GOLDEN BESTSELLER PRIZE, SERBIA, 2004 - THE ALCHEMIST--CORINE INTERNATIONAL AWARD FOR BEST FICTION, GERMANY, 2002 - CLUB OF BUDAPEST PLANETARY ARTS AWARD, HUNGARY, 2002 - BAMBI AWARD, GERMANY, 2001 - XXIII PREMIO INTERNAZIONALE FREGENE, ITALY, 2001 - CRYSTAL MIRROR AWARD, POLAND, 2000 - CHEVALIER DE L'ORDRE NATIONAL DE LA LÉGION D'HONNEUR, FRANCE, 1999 - WORLD ECONOMIC FORUM CRYSTAL AWARD, 1999- GOLDEN MEDAL OF GALICIA, SPAIN, 1999- THE FIFTH MOUNTAIN--INTERNATIONAL IMPAC LITERARY AWARD FINALIST, IRELAND, 2000 - THE VALKYRIES: AN ENCOUNTER WITH ANGELS--INTERNATIONAL IMPAC LITERARY AWARD FINALIST, IRELAND, 1997

COMENDADOR DE ORDEM DO RIO BRANCO, BRAZIL, 1998 - GOLDEN BOOK AWARD, YUGOSLAVIA, 1995–2000 AND 2004 SUPER GRINZANE CAVOUR BOOK AWARD, ITALY, 1996 - FLAIANO INTERNATIONAL AWARD, ITALY, 1996 - KNIGHT OF ARTS AND LETTERS, FRANCE, 1996 - ELLE GRAND PRIX LITTERAIRE DES LECTRICES, FRANCE, 1995 - UNITED NATIONS MESSENGER OF PEACE, 2007 - AMBASSADOR OF EUROPEAN UNION FOR INTERCULTURAL DIALOGUE, 2008 - UNESCO SPECIAL COUNSELOR FOR INTERCULTURAL DIALOGUES AND SPIRITUAL CONVERGENCES

The Alchemist is the only book that I read three times in my life. The first two times were back to back. My uncle gave me that book, saying that it was interesting. That was 25 years ago. I read it, for the first time, because I wanted an escape from my classes, everything was a better alternative than to study.

I was surprised by how easy it was to read. The words were simple and the story, straight forward. I finished the book within days. Then, I felt that something was missing, so I went through it a second time. The first time, I got the story. The second time I got the essence.

Without disclosing the core of the book, I will tell you that that book started the rewriting process of my mindset.

"Perfection is a lie."
Dr Bak Nguyen

I only wrote that quote 22 years later, but the concept started after the second time I read the Alchemist. Since wealth is in the journey, what kind of good can perfection bring to the table?

The journey is the essence. The journey is the treasure. Until that point, everything was goal-driven to me. At school, the teachers were process-driven. That wasn't the journey either. Can a goal be perfect? Hardly if that goal has been reached. Perfection only exists in the narrative written and edited after the facts.

"On paper, perfection is king, not in life."
Dr Bak Nguyen

A process, any process, can be perfected. If one spends long enough to polish it, it might get closer to perfection, but what is a process but a tool? Some times a real tool, other times, a tool for the mind, a mindset. How long should one polish his tools before making use of them?

I've been raised to respect my tools. I keep them clean and in order. Some times I even gave them names. Ever heard the saying: "To anyone holding a hammer, everything looks like a nail?" That's what a tool can do to you. It is just that, a tool. Respect them, and eventually, you will have to let them go to yield new ones.

It took me nearly 2 decades later to finally break that curse of possession and blind loyalty. I finally unburdened myself and my luggage. I got rid of my emotional luggage and past tools, medals and regrets. I learned to let all of them go, without distinction. To move forward, one needs a light and kind heart, not one burden with the past.

He may not have written it within those exact words, but that's the essence I got from his masterpiece, **THE ALCHEMIST**. And what will happen at the end of the journey? Well, another one will begin. That's life, but not as I've been taught. If Life is a river, we've been trained to live close by.

We all live from the resources that the river brings. The strongest amongst us will learn to swim in the river to catch the bigger fishes. Some will even be strong enough to swim against the waves, but not for long. Every time, **Pride** will lead us to failure as we were trying to beat the river. And then, we used our brains and built dams! Until we got caught by the flood following.

"Don't mess with the flow if you are not ready
to clean up the mess from the flood."
Dr Bak Nguyen

The story of the river can be the story of our entire lifetime or only simply your chapter 1. It is for us to choose. Will the river win the battle? Absolutely. If we had any success, it was momentarily. Even the dam will not last forever. Do you see any perfection in that story? Even anything that will come close to perfection?

Instead, from our momentary victory, we built Pride and false confidence, forgetting the essence of the real story: Harmony. Perfection is not harmony, if anything, perfection will blind you from your quest to find harmony and happiness.

Going back to the river, Nature will always win, if you look far enough in time. The definition of perfection was based and defined upon a short time frame, on which arrogance and ignorance made us believe that we were winning.

Take the example that you wish, I can show you how obsolete perfection becomes, if not sooner, than later. Life is dynamic, the only thing one can do is to go with its flow, that's called harmony. Harmony is the adaptation of one to its environment.

Harmony is not just wisdom, it is strength and speed all in one. Since I find no merit swimming against the flow nor to try to stand still in the water, I freed much resources to learn to swim, to run, to surf and to fly instead. That's where it all started, from the day I dropped perfection and understood that there are many journeys.

From Paulo Coelho's wisdom, not just life, but even the treasures were found within the dynamic, so why even bother about pride and perfection? Harmony, not perfection! Harmony of the journey, harmony in the process, harmony with the goal. That is what we should aim for.

It will take more than 2 decades for me to understand fully his wisdom, but that day, 25 years ago, Paulo Coelho freed me from the **TRACKS OF PERFECTION**. Today, I am known as a bold driver and a free thinker. I am bold because I am free. I am free because I am sensitive to the world and the people around me.

Necessary evil, collateral damage are all work products of, either ignorance or from the pride to refuse to see passed perfection, that beyond, there is harmony. And the beauty of it, is that I am not talking about compromise, but not at all.

I am talking about harmony, to be one with the flow. Yes, things will change. Things are changing as we speak. Refuse to adapt and you will become obsolete soon enough. Look ahead and adapt and you will evolve.

You do your best with what you have, that's it! The alternative is either to miss that window of opportunity or to stay paralyzed for life, just like the owner of the small restaurant on the way to the Mecca (in **THE ALCHEMIST**).

That image stayed engrave in my mind. It reminds me that Life is not a journey. All of our journeys will compound to what our life will be. Until the endpoint, there is always a new journey to jump on to.

Because I understood the myriad of journeys, I let go of the pressure and the lies of perfection. Without perfection, Pride lost all of its grip on me. It did not make any sense anymore. I got rid of **Pride** too! The void left allowed me to look beyond the noise and the fog, so I understood harmony and, eventually, understood abundance.

From **JOURNEYS** to **ABUNDANCE**, it is a big stretch, but if I was not freed by Paulo, that will have never happened. To a mentor that I never met, one who shape my destiny to freedom, thank you Paulo Coelho.

I recommend, to each of you looking for their place in the world, looking for your name, to start your quest of Identity with **THE ALCHEMIST**. I, myself, have written many books on the matter, but by far, the most elegant is Paulo's.

If you have interests, here are my titles in which you will find answers on your Quest of Identity:

IDENTITY -004
THE ANTHOLOGY OF QUESTS
BY Dr BAK NGUYEN

HYBRID -011
THE MODERN QUEST OF IDENTITY
BY Dr BAK NGUYEN

012 - **REBOOT**
MIDLIFE CRISIS
BY Dr BAK NGUYEN

015 - **FORCES OF NATURE**
FORGING THE CHARACTER
OF WINNERS
BY Dr BAK NGUYEN

049 - **MINDSET ARMORY**
BY Dr BAK NGUYEN

"One's legend can only start the day one is out of his or her quest of identity."

Dr Bak Nguyen

This is why **THE ALCHEMIST** by Paulo Coelho is first on my list of books of the **BOOTCAMP**. Find out who you are and what you are made of. Only then, you can know where to go and what to do. Once out of your Quest of Identity, it is not easier, it is clearer,. That alone will speeds things up!

From **MILLION DOLLAR MINDSET,** this is **BOOTCAMP: 8 BOOKS TO REWRITE MINDSETS INTO WINNING STATES OF MIND.** Welcome to the **ALPHAS**.

Dr BAK NGUYEN

CHAPTER 2

RICH DAD POOR DAD
FROM ROBERT KIYOSAKI
AND SHARON LECHTER

by Dr BAK NGUYEN

ROBERT KIYOSAKI, American businessman and author, founder of Rich Global LLC and the Rich Dad Company. Author of more than 26 books, including the international best seller RICH DAD POOR DAD series, translated into 51 languages and sold over 41 million copies worldwide.

SHARON LECHTER, elite entrepreneur, philanthropist, founder and CEO of Pay Your Family First, a financial education organization. In 1997 Sharon co-authored the international bestseller RICH DAD POOR DAD, along with 14 other books in the Rich Dad series. Over 10 years as CEO she led the Rich Dad Company and brand into an international powerhouse. In 2008 she was asked by the Napoleon Hill Foundation to help re-energize the powerful teachings of NAPOLEON HILL just as the international economy was faltering. She has released three bestselling books in cooperation with the Foundation.

IN 2008 SHARON WAS APPOINTED TO THE FIRST PRESIDENT OF THE UNITED STATES ADVISORY COUNCIL ON FINANCIAL LITERACY. THE COUNCIL SERVED BOTH PRESIDENT BUSH AND PRESIDENT OBAMA ADVISING THEM ON THE NEED FOR FINANCIAL LITERACY EDUCATION. IN 2002, CHILDHELP HONORED SHARON AND HER HUSBAND, MICHAEL, AS RECIPIENTS OF THE SPIRIT OF THE CHILDREN AWARD. IN 2004, SHARON AND MICHAEL WERE RECOGNIZED AS AN ARIZONA "POWER COUPLE," AND SHARON WAS ALSO NAMED AS A 2005 WOMAN OF DISTINCTION BY THE CROHN'S & COLITIS FOUNDATION OF AMERICA. SHE WAS HONORED WITH A 2012 POSITIVELY POWERFUL WOMEN AWARD FOR PHILANTHROPIC LEADERSHIP, BY THE PHOENIX BUSINESS JOURNAL AS ONE OF 2013'S 25 DYNAMIC WOMEN IN BUSINESS, AND MOST RECENTLY HONORED BY NATIONAL BANK OF ARIZONA WITH THE 2013 WOMAN OF THE YEAR AWARD AND ARIZONA BUSINESS MAGAZINE AS ONE OF THE 50 MOST INFLUENTIAL WOMEN IN ARIZONA BUSINESS

I was freed, but then, I still need to know where to go and how to build. I found out about Robert Kiyosaki from the book he co-wrote with Donald Trump, later to become President Trump, President of the United States of America.

Looking for my ways, after graduation, after turning my back on the Hollywood opportunity, drowning in regrets and debts as I opened my first clinic, I discovered the books of Donald Trump. Very bold, very shocking, it made me realize that life and business are more than meet the eye.

Then, I stumbled upon **WHY WE WANT YOU TO BE RICH**. It is then that I discovered Robert Kiyosaki. His landmark book is **RICH DAD POOR DAD** with co-author Sharon Lechter. I bought that one and read it.

What an easy read, telling the story from the perspective of an 8-year-old confronted with the contrary instructions from his 2 dads: one who never finished high school and died as the richest man of the state of Hawaï; the other, the superintendent for education of the state of Hawaï, a man referred to as his poor dad.

Well, that resonated much with me, since I am from an immigrant family deeply rooted in the value of education. That also sounded insulting to my education background and training. By the time I discover Robert, I was already a doctor and was way passed my credential and the Pride. I was looking for answers, real answers.

I read the book within a few hours. Then, I bought the audio version and went through a second time with Tranie, my newly wedded wife. We were both lost and shocked by Robert story in Sharon's words. I was supposed to be good in finance, but all I could get was debts, more and more debts, in the hundreds of thousands of dollars. Well, one single line from **RICH DAD POOR DAD** made all the difference in my world:

"An asset is what will feed you.
A liability is what will eat you."
Robert Kiyosaki

The book is so much more than that, but that line rewrote entirely my code and my DNA at my core. I was investing heavily, but I could not figure out why I kept sinking. The only metrics I had to success was the checks I had to sign to pay my taxes and the fact that the banks were willing to lend me more and more.

To understand feeding from eating, without but, was mind-opening, to both Tranie and I. To that point, we were life and business partner for 10 years already, but our common education started with the comprehension of the definition of **ASSET** and **LIABILITY**.

From there, we took massive actions to change our current situation. We leveraged ourselves even more to buy assets. To that point, we noticed that assets are mostly what we disregarded while we, all of us, have such a tendency to love the liabilities and to hold them dearly close to our hearts.

I am not saying that I am liability-free today, I am simply saying that I know what is what, and the labels are pretty bold. That was the beginning of our rise as a power couple. We built up our businesses and bought real estates.

For our first 10 years in business, we were looking to reach a million, then, to become millionaires. Well, we are multimillionaires today, and we never saw the day that it happened, we were too busy closing our next deal! The key was to have the right mindset and to act as **WE**, as a team.

On that, please take my advice. If you wanted to succeed and to be happy, well, get your partner involved and share with him or her your plans and your ambitions. Only when both of you are on the same page that you can have it all: wealth, success and happiness!

And you know what? Becoming a millionaire was much easier and smoother than when we were fighting tooth and nail for bites and left overs! I am not saying easy, but easier! Easier because we now know the difference between eating and feeding!

Much later, I will dwell on the concept of liability to define my next level: leverage. To Robert and Sharon, I will eternally be grateful, they have opened my eyes to read finance and to finally have the wording right.

Unfortunately, the everyday wording is very confusing, some times, misleading.

That day I awoke from the lies of false wording, I noticed the chains around my mind and myself. Applying the wording of Robert and Sharon, I undid the knots one after the next, to rebuild a different web, one on which I today stand, talking with men who created billions in value.

Four single words, well applied, changed my life: **ASSET**, **LIABILITY**, **EATING** and **FEEDING**. I recommend **RICH DAD POOR DAD** to anyone at any age. The sooner the better, since what you will learn in that book is how to fix your mistakes, but even better, to build without making mistakes!

Where ever you are in life, read that book. It is a few hours of your life that will save your years and decades of misery. I wish I wrote that book, but I am so glad that Robert and Sharon did.

41 million copies sold! That means that there are 41 million lives that changed, almost overnight! And that was from a few hours reading a great book written in

simple words, powerful words. Robert, Sharon, thank you so much to have shared.

On that, I received an email a few years back, from a patient I treated a while ago. He wrote to me from another province, thanking me to have changed his life. He enjoyed so much the new smile I gave him, but he also added how grateful he was to me as I influenced him to grow and to build. Today, he is a successful entrepreneur and real estate owner.

It was very pleasant to read, but I could not recall what I said to him to have marked his imagination as such… then I remembered, I told him, as a farewell note, to read **RICH DAD POOR DAD**! That book did not just change my life, it helped also those I recommended it to.

So how come, not all who read that book have experienced the same transformation? I believe it is a matter of how open and ready you are to change your old ways.

"Habits die hard. Mindsets are much more stubborn than habits."
Dr Bak Nguyen

A warning note, to everyone who will be reading that book, be aware that the initial shock will twist your mind upside down and will make you feel like you are drowning. That's good, that's because you've understood something, that you've have touched the essence. Give yourself some space and ask yourself the right question: is that an asset or a liability, without but, without if?

I knew what I was from my **Quest of Identity**. I gained **CLARITY**. Now, I know what to choose and why. Things are getting easier and smoother. Together with Tranie, we rose to new heights.

I told you that I decided to write this book as my new protege asked me questions about how to change one's mindset. He also asked me about the universal laws of the universe and how did I apply them to further my growth. Well, knowing the difference between an asset and a liability was the basic of one of those universal laws…

The next phase is to understand that an asset and a liability are one and the same, only in a different phase of the cycle. Life is dynamic, remember?

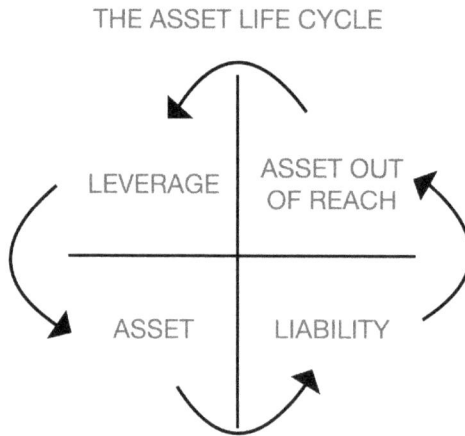

THE ASSET LIFE CYCLE

LEVERAGE | ASSET OUT OF REACH

ASSET | LIABILITY

This I understood as I discovered the means of leverage. Any asset has a life circle where it will eventually turn into a liability. Now, Robert and Sharon's concept make even more sense!

The reason why we love so much our liabilities is that we see the potential in them. In Robert's words, it's about feeding or eating you at that exact moment. But some liabilities, once grown will grow into assets, if you took good care of them.

Most liabilities have the potential to grow into an asset, you need to invest time, energy and money to cultivate them. As you have outgrown yourself to take care of an asset outside of your reach, that will eventually become a leverage, base solely of the fact of your growth consequential from your investment taking care of the liability.

Take the example of the woman taking care of her child (**liability**) will grow into a mother (**leverage**) and, one day the child will become a man or woman (**asset**). Eventually, the man and woman will grow old and become a liability to his children. That's a cycle, the life cycle of an asset.

An asset, no matter what it is, will slowly fade into a less valuable asset and eventually become a liability. That liability can either die or eventually be recycled into a potential.

"Asset and liability are two faces of the same coin."
Dr Bak Nguyen

At every point in time, to ask the question of **EATING** or **FEEDING** will shed the light of the present status of an asset, without but, without if. One line, one single line from Robert and Sharon gave me the key to understand part of the universe.

I already told you how **PERFECTION** is a lie, follow the logic of the Life cycle of an asset, how long will you have to polish a liability until it becomes an asset? And then, will you be able to let it go as the same asset you've polished for years turns into a liability? Why would you ever let it go, now that you've spent years and tears to polish it into perfection? That's your downfall, right there!

Always ask yourself that question of **IS IT FEEDING YOU ARE EATING YOU**? And act accordingly. It is okay to have liabilities. It is normal to love your liabilities, we all do. But don't bet your house on your liabilities! That is what I am trying to tell you! Know the label and its expiration dates before applying theorems and strategies to them.

"An asset is what feed you. A liability is what eat you."
Robert Kiyosaki

Because it is of such prime importance to choose the right pieces on which to build from and to understand the dynamic coming with it, I recommend reading **RICH DAD POOR DAD** written by Robert Kiyosaki and Sharon Lechter, as the second book of the **BOOTCAMP**.

In **THE ALCHEMIST**, you understood **WHY. RICH DAD POOR DAD** will show you the **WHAT**.

From **MILLION DOLLAR MINDSET,** this is **BOOTCAMP: 8 BOOKS TO REWRITE MINDSETS INTO WINNING STATES OF MIND.** Welcome to the **ALPHAS**.

Dr BAK NGUYEN

CHAPTER 3

THE COMPOUND EFFECT
FROM DARREN HARDY
by Dr BAK NGUYEN

DARREN HARDY, publisher of SUCCESS magazine and Success Media, Executive producer and master distributor of The People's Network (TPN), and president of The Success Training Network (TSTN). Darren Hardy is most known for his popular book "The Compound Effect" that is still quoted by top critics as his best work to date. Author of three books:

- THE COMPOUND EFFECT, 2010
- LIVING YOUR BEST YEAR EVER, 2011
- THE ENTREPRENEUR ROLLER COASTER, 2015

AWARDED THE 'MASTER OF INFLUENCE' DESIGNATION BY THE NATIONAL SPEAKERS ASSOCIATION (NSA) IN HONOR OF HIS PROFESSIONALISM IN PUBLIC SPEAKING.

In this **BOOTCAMP**, to rewrite your mindsets into winning states of mind, we went through the **WHY** with **THE ALCHEMIST** and the **WHAT** with **RICH DAD POOR DAD**. Now, let's focus on the every day, the **HOW**.

On that matter, the book that came to my mind instantly is **THE COMPOUND EFFECT** by Darren Hardy. It is a very great read and will help any of you to go from point A to point B.

"Compound interest is the
8th wonder of the world."
Albert Einstein

Following this line of thoughts, Darren Hardy dwells into us the power of repetition and resilience. That power, everyone has, no matter where you are stationed and what your conditions are, you can start turning your life around with this simple incrementation: to compound your effort, day after day.

Out of respect for Darren, I won't summarize the book. I just gave you the synopsis of the title. That being said, there is a great passage in that book that, even 10 years later, I can still remember clearly.

Darren mentioned that he was tired of going out and decided to stay in, in an evening. He was rich, single, handsome, but was a little tired of the dating scene, the empty spark and the meanless encounters. He wanted something of substance for a change.

He got a bottle of wine. Near the fireplace, started writing about his perfect lady companion. He enjoyed the process so much that he wrote 5 pages, front and back, about the woman of his dream. When he stopped, he was happy and depress all at once. Everything was clear, clear that the woman of his dream does not exist!

A few years later, Darren got married, to the woman he painted with his words that night. To know how it happened, you will have to read his story, it is not mine to tell. The essence here is that it is possible to reach for whatever you set your mind at, even to marry the perfect partner!

That story made me laugh as I was listening to it, driving from Montreal to Toronto. Tranie and I were already married. She was napping in the passenger chair. I woke her up and replayed the chapter. We both picked up on the essence of the story and employed Darren's recipe for personal and professional growth. The rest is History in the becoming.

Today, both her mentors and mine have created or managed billion and hundreds of billions of dollars. Hundreds of billions, I am not even sure how many zeroes that is! The point is that we applied Darren's recipe to attract mentors and opportunities to us. And you know what? It is working!

All of my mentors said to us how pleasant it is to spend time with us. This is coming from men that we could have read about from books or from articles in Times, Forbes or Success Magazine. Those people are like you and I, only, they thrive for excellence, every day.

One time, one mentor even thanked me to have taken the role of his protege. I was astonished, I should be the one thanking him, and I did! My point here is how well the attraction worked.

"Leadership attracts leadership."
Christian Trudeau

One other time, as I was preparing to run for office, as my country was in a crisis and needed me, I trained with Dr Benkhalifa. We had an intense day going through history and its injustices. Then, just after dinner, he told me to read a book about management.

I went on Apple Books and download the audiobook. I went through the chapters before falling asleep listening to that book. By the next morning, I was halfway through. My mentor couldn't believe that I executed as fast, although I was exhausted.

I finished that book before the end of our weekend Bootcamp. I must say that I did not learn much from that book and reported that. He smiled. He told me how special I was, but it is not my intelligence that will make my legend, but my resilience.

Fun fact, I downloaded the book because I needed the distraction. Going through History and social injustices were draining my energy and morale, a book on business management was a better alternative.

Then, as I got upset that the book did not contain any new and rich information, I used it to debate with my mentor, finally giving me an upper hand in our conversation. That last part, I did not share with him, but I surely enjoyed the rest of the conversation that went between the both of us. That's a Bootcamp to remember in the National Capital city.

Resilience and discipline, in time, will forge any person into an athlete and a champion. Repetition and Will will forge any mind into a thinker and a leader. It is not just about doing the same thing day in and day out, but about doing it a little better, a little more. And if you are like me, if you like to sprint, well, you will have to keep that speed and to accelerate from there!

I never had to run for office, the problem solved itself before I had the chance to jump in. Boy, I was relieved, I wasn't doing it out of ambition, but out of duty… and by now, you must know how lazy I am.

I kept that habit of running and accelerating from my own speed. A few years later, I wrote **MOMENTUM TRANSFER** with co-author coach Dino Masson, sharing with the world how I built my Momentum and speed: from repetition and consistency… with a little touch of ambition and playfulness.

I started my writing career trying to write a TED talk. I was counting the words to match the length of the presentation. I finished writing that book within 2 weeks. I went from counting the words to count the chapters instead.

Then, I started to count the books instead of counting the chapters. Funny things, my words expanded within the chapters and my books set me up on the world's stage, setting world records, one after the next.

I started writing a book with William to keep my promise as a dad. One chapter at a time, one story after the next, together, my 8-year-old son and I, we wrote 8 children books within a month. History will tell that to celebrate a world record, we scored 3 more!

With William's help, I broke the **sound barrier**, going from the average of writing a book a month (15 on 15) to 2 books a month… from the beginning (36 books over 18 months + 1 week). That world record was set 3 months later!

The titles are bold and the story, well, impressive, but on the ground, we were just father and son having fun connecting, writing one chapter at a time, each day, day after day. Eventually, we speeded up and kept the pace. It was fun, it was pleasant, it was smooth.

And that's what a Momentum is, a smooth force of change. Just like compound interests, little by little, the effect is growing up and, eventually, the math won't make sense anymore. I am still not counting in the hundreds of billions, not even the billions, but the plans are set and in motion. Just like the day I reached the millionaire status, I might miss the day the billion will happen, being too busy accelerating. That's the state of mind!

There is one tremendous upside with that state of mind: often we are off between our goals and its delays. Well, that state of mind accelerating and not looking back has the tremendous advantage to never disappoint since we are always looking forward and scoring.

Just like I missed the mark of the millionaire when it happened, I also missed the mark of writing a million words. I was somewhere in confinement, in the midst of the COVID war. I only noticed the milestone 3 books later, as the computer compiled 1.1 million words written!

And to tell you the truth, I am not forcing nor beating myself at the task. Hell no! I am doing that as a hobby on top of my existing duties as CEO changing the world while attending to my patients. If **FUN** and **CONNECTION** was my ingredient to the recipe of Momentum, I started from Darren's formula, compounding the actions on the ground.

His love story made such an impact on me that it removed all the doubts I might have about my quest. Darren, thank you for sharing and for your inspiration with such charisma.

You have the **WHY**, the **WHAT** and now, you have the **HOW**. Are you ready for change? Are you ready to change? Where to? Is for you to decide. How? Trust me, there aren't many recipes for success universally accessible out there, Darren's formula is a sure bet!

For that reason, **THE COMPOUND EFFECT**, written by Darren Hardy is the third book on my list of the **BOOTCAMP** to rewrite your mindsets into winning states of mind. And if you are lazy like me, well, go grab the audiobook, it is very entertaining!

From **MILLION DOLLAR MINDSET,** this is **BOOTCAMP: 8 BOOKS TO REWRITE MINDSETS INTO WINNING STATES OF MIND.** Welcome to the **ALPHAS**.

Dr BAK NGUYEN

CHAPTER 4

THIS IS YOUR TIME
FROM JOEL OSTEEN
by Dr BAK NGUYEN

JOEL SCOTT OSTEEN, American pastor, superstar televangelist, and best-selling author. Included on Barbara Walters's list of the 10 Most Fascinating People of 2006. Authors of 15 books.

- YOUR BEST LIFE NOW: 7 STEPS TO LIVING AT YOUR FULL POTENTIAL (2004)
- BECOME A BETTER YOU: 7 KEYS TO IMPROVING YOUR LIFE EVERY DAY (2007)
- YOUR BEST LIFE BEGINS EACH MORNING: DEVOTIONS TO START EVERY DAY OF THE YEAR (2008)
- GOOD, BETTER, BLESSED: LIVING WITH PURPOSE, POWER AND PASSION (2008)
- HOPE FOR TODAY BIBLE (2009)
- IT'S YOUR TIME : ACTIVATE YOUR FAITH, ACHIEVE YOUR DREAMS, AND INCREASE IN GOD'S FAVOR (2009)
- LIVING IN FAVOR, ABUNDANCE AND JOY (2010)
- EVERY DAY A FRIDAY: HOW TO BE HAPPIER 7 DAYS A WEEK (2011)
- I DECLARE: 31 PROMISES TO SPEAK OVER YOUR LIFE (2012)
- BREAK OUT!: 5 KEYS TO GO BEYOND YOUR BARRIERS AND LIVE AN EXTRAORDINARY LIFE (2013)
- YOU CAN, YOU WILL: 8 UNDENIABLE QUALITIES OF A WINNER (2014)
- THE POWER OF I AM: TWO WORDS THAT WILL CHANGE YOUR LIFE TODAY (2015)
- THINK BETTER, LIVE BETTER: A VICTORIOUS LIFE BEGINS IN YOUR MIND (2016)
- BLESSED IN THE DARKNESS: HOW ALL THINGS ARE WORKING FOR YOUR GOOD (2017)
- NEXT LEVEL THINKING: 10 POWERFUL THOUGHTS FOR A SUCCESSFUL AND ABUNDANT LIFE (2018)

I have a golden rule: to always finish the book once I started reading it. Over the years, that rule caused me much pain on certain titles… which took years for me to finish. So I learned to be very selective before engaging in a book.

Then, I started opening up more and more. As I discovered the audiobook format, I was much more inclined to give it a try. I remember once, going to Barnes & Noble and buying a copy of each of the audiobooks they have in store. Biography, finance, personal growth, the only ones I did not touch were the fictional stuff.

I loved audiobooks, since they kept me company on my road trips, driving from one city to the next for business. The average duration of my trip was 3-6 hours drive, the distance between Montreal - New York, Boston and Toronto. These were my frequent destinations.

There is more to life than work, my wife reminded me. This time, we would take off for the Caribbean Sun, in Punta Cana for a week off, doing, well, nothing!

Nothing?! How insecure I can be facing that word?! By that time, I haven't started to write yet, so I was looking for a good reading. **THIS IS YOUR TIME** was on my shelf for a little while by now. Well, ok, I guess that the time is right.

But now, I have an issue, I bought the CD version and going to PUNTA CANA, well, I won't be driving. Without thinking twice, I went online and bought the digital version. I had it downloaded and ready on my iPhone for the flight and, maybe for the beach, looking at the clouds. I was getting warmed to the idea of vacations.

On the plane, I started the book but fell asleep by half of the first chapter. I woke up when it was time to deplane. Then, we got through custom, transportation and check-in. At the hotel, there were the services, the resorts, the pools, the buffets and the multiple restaurants. It took me 2 days before I could sit on the beach with nothing to do!

And nothing, that was my clue to continue my reading of **THIS IS YOUR TIME**. To that point, I have no idea of who Joel Osteen was, I just read the back of the ALBUM and it seems interesting. Well, by the 4th chapter, I understood who Joel Osteen was: a pastor!

Never in my life, I would have bought a book from a pastor! I spent part of my childhood in church listening to sermons of priests… The bible, I know pretty well, and the priests, I have little interests for their opinions or interpretations.

But I was stuck with my stupid rule: to finish the book I started! The next one in line was a book by Richard Branson I was dying to start but not before finishing this one first! I was trapped to listen to the sermons of a pastor who I bought twice his book!

My only consolation was that I had the beach and the sun to keep me company. Tranie laughed so hard when she understood what I was up to with my **NOTHING TIME**!

Well, I started this chapter saying that I paid dearly some of my poor choices. This time, I was in for a treat, little did I know that this rule will have me rewrite my vision of life.

I was in for now 2 days and nearly at the core of the book, when, on a beautiful afternoon, the belly facing the sun, a pina colada in hand, I experienced revelation. Out of respect for Joel Osteen, I will not summarize the book. I will just borrow one passage that changed my life entirely. This is how it goes:

We are all going to die someday. Well, the day we die, we will face Saint-Peter at the gates of heaven. On the way to our final trial, we will follow Saint-Peter through the halls of Heaven. On each side of the hall are doors, many doors, with names on them. Eventually, we will pass by a door with our name written on.

- Saint-Peter, is that my name?
- Yup.
- Can I open the door?
- Nope.

But curiosity will eat us up and we will be begging Saint-Peter. Please, please, pleeeease! At that point, we even forgot that we are dead and on the way to our trial. Finally, Saint-Peter will take pity on us:

- If you insisted, be my guest. But I have to warn you that there is nothing of interest for you behind those doors.

Ignoring the warning, we will rush on these doors. Surprisingly, what was a single door has somehow changed into double doors as we push them wide open. On the other side, shells and shells of gifts, wrapped with love and attention will greet us. If you saw the warehouse of Santa Claus, well, this is the Supersized version of it.

Bouncing of joy, we get closer and look at the gifts: on each single one, only one name is written, ours. Big, small, gigantic, they are all labeled to us. Smiling, we will turn back to Saint-Peter:

- Are those all for me?
- Yup.
- Can I open them?
- Nope. They are useless now.
- What are they?
- These were the blessing intended for you while you were on earth. But since you never asked for them, well, what a waste!

And with that, we will be walking to our judgement day, our trial.

Well, Joel said, I want my the doors of my warehouse in heaven to be emptied the day I will walk these halls. I want everything to be sold out and gone since I will be welcoming all of the blessings God intended for me! Who am I to refuse God's gifts?

Those words opened my eyes about **ABUNDANCE**. To this point, I was praying to say thank you or to ask for forgiveness. I wasn't asking for blessings, not to bother God. Well, that story changed everything.

How ungrateful are we as we refused the gifts and good intentions? All these gifts are wrapped with love and dedication, from God! It would not only be a waste to refuse them, it would be arrogance to decline what God gave!

I know, I know, nothing is free! Everything that I received, I will have to deliver on. That story I know by heart. But why deprive myself of the gifts, with more toys and more talents, it will be more fun, and once I have fun, well, I can score all day long!

This is the wisdom I learned from Joel Osteen that day, sitting on the beach and enjoying my **NOTHING TIME**! That was 10 years ago.

Today, I know the **WAY TO ABUNDANCE**, I received the gifts of love, of healing, people and myself, of speed and of attraction. Those were the first gifts I unwrapped. Then, I received my wings back and, just at the corner of the table, I unwrapped the talent of writing at world record pace.

I took each of my gifts for a long test drive and have to grow to master them and to yield their power for good. Yes, I am having fun and I am delivering on each of the gifts that I have received. I know they are still so many wrapped up there, all custom made for me.

I also never forgot the other golden rule of giving and receiving. To be able to receive more, you must give, at an even greater amount. And this is what I am doing sharing with you, writing books and embracing the cameras and the stages. I am not giving back, I am giving forward.

In my past books on the QUEST OF IDENTITY, **FORCES OF NATURE** and **MINDSET ARMORY**, I mentioned that we receive swords, armors and shields as gifts. They will be useful for a while, and eventually, we will have to clean them up and to leave them behind for someone else to find and to yield. That's how God set the **CYCLE OF GRATITUDE**.

If one isn't sharing and keep his or her gifts, well, he or she will not be available to receive more. **SCARCITY** will take over his heart and he might walk in **ABUNDANCE** without ever knowing it, blinded by an old helmet.

This is not Joel, it is me talking. But Joel showed me the way, the **WAY TO ABUNDANCE**.

We learned about the multiple journeys with Paulo Coelho. Then, we learned what to bet on and how with Robert Kiyosaki and Sharon Lechter. Darren Hardy showed us how to yield any power, any wish we have. Well, Joel just showed us the armory where to find powers and blessings.

I could have started this journey showing you the **WAREHOUSES OF HEAVEN**, you would be excited about them, but you won't be ready to ask and to receive. This is why so many warehouse are stocked at full capacity up there!

Now, now you are ready to ask and to receive. Now you are ready to give to receive. Find your journey, the next one. Know your assets from your liabilities and bet on the right ones and nurture the others until you have outgrown them to leverage them as assets.

Whatever you want, you can have, incrementing it today, a small action at the time. One action after the next, day after day will compound into the momentum you couldn't imagine. So now, you are ready for more. For this reason, **THIS IS YOUR TIME** written by Joel Osteen is the 4th book on the list of **THE BOOTCAMP**.

Joel, you could have given me a million dollar, that would not have made me as wealthy than to share this knowledge with me. On my **WAY TO ABUNDANCE**, I found my powers, my blessing, but more importantly, I found purpose.

Joel Osteen, from the bottom of my heart, thank you.

From **MILLION DOLLAR MINDSET,** this is **BOOTCAMP: 8 BOOKS TO REWRITE MINDSETS INTO WINNING STATES OF MIND.** Welcome to the **ALPHAS**.

Dr BAK NGUYEN

PART II

CHAPTER 5

THE SECOND COMING OF STEVE JOBS
FROM ALAN DEUTSCHMAN

by Dr BAK NGUYEN

ALAN DEUTSCHMAN, journalist, Silicon Valley correspondent for Fortune, senior writer at Fast Company, "Profit Motive" columnist for GQ, contributing editor at Vanity Fair and New York Magazine.

Authors of 5 books, his books have been translated into eight languages:

- THE SECOND COMING OF STEVE JOBS (2000)
- A TALE OF TWO VALLEYS (2003)
- CHANGE OR DIE (2007)
- WALK THE WALK (2009)
- HOW STEVE JOBS CHANGED OUR WORLD (2011)

I told you that I was not a You Tuber reviewing lens and cameras. **BOOTCAMP** is my way to honor my mentors, those I haven't met in real life yet. Only Now, after completing PART I, I realize how powerful this book really is. It retraces the step of my rise and how I found my powers.

If this book is powerful, it is from the **POWER OF GRATITUDE**. Never forget that to receive more, you must give. To receive more, you must accept gracefully, to receive more, you must be open. To receive more, you must be generous.

This is basically what I took 71 books to tell you, using more than 1.1 million words, and will keep going on. Why? Because it is fun and easy; because in **ABUNDANCE**, we count to know, to brag and to empower others to do even more.

Yield the **POWER OF GRATITUDE** and walk your **WAY TO ABUNDANCE.** Some will take days to start, other, weeks, others years. It is okay, to each our own pace. This was about finding our happiness. That's the conclusion of PART I.

So what about PART II? Well, if you are like most of us, even if you feel empowered and ready to face the entire universe, we still need support and the insurance that others have walked the path before us. The great news is they are many of them.

They not only walked their **WAY TO ABUNDANCE**, but they have done so so boldly that words and books trailed behind them, even if some are not anymore from this life.

PART II is dedicated to the people who walked the path and wrote boldly their story and destiny, inspiring and touching so many of us. STEVE JOBS is by far, the person who has shown me the way, being himself, without compromise.

Over the years, I read many books written about Steve Jobs, the co-founder of **Apple Computer**, the owner of **PIXAR** and the visionary who got the phones smart! He has changed the world more than once, even now, as he is no more, his vision still shapes the way we communicate and interact, we do business and learn, we envision the world and the future.

Ok, he is one of my idols. But it was thanks to the work and through the words fo Alan Deutschman that I had the chance to really understand who Steve Jobs was, and to experience the world walking in his shoes.

THE SECOND COMING OF STEVE JOBS is an unauthorized biography written in the early 2000s, as Steve Jobs was back at Apple after more than a decade in exile. And this was before Steve Jobs invented **SMART** and put it into the iPhone.

The only way to experience life through Steve Jobs' dark times is to read the words and the chapter, from his disgrace to his rise, a second time to glory and power. It is common wisdom that we learn more from our mistakes than from our successes. This is our way to learn from the mistakes of Steve Jobs, but moreover, to learn how to not give up and how to come back from a fall.

Journeys, we all have. Challenges, we all face. The difference between a story and a great one is how the hero reacts to a challenge greater than him or herself. This is the essence of **THE SECOND COMING OF STEVE JOBS**.

If you have made it once, it might be out of luck, the naysayers will say. But making it big, twice, this is no coincidence. And we all know the rest of the story, in the 2000s, within a decade, Steve Jobs reinvented the world more than once, erasing everything before, even his own success and failures.

So if, and I am only saying IF, Steve Jobs was lucky the first time, his real training and the forging of his mindset happened within the 10 years that he fell from the spotlight. He was still very powerful, but he was hurt, and then, he outgrew his pain and liabilities.

I got that book as a gift from Tranie. This was before I discovered the audiobooks format. We were still a young couple newly wedded and living our honeymoon phase. I was a true Steve Jobs' fan, everything Apple sales, I had at least one copy.

My love story with Apple and Steve Jobs started back in dental school as I was struggling to get my first movie out on time for the National Dental Conferences. I discovered the power of the MAC as Steve Jobs was declaring war to Jeffrey Katzenberg,

Disney executive who will eventually leave to co-found **DREAMWORKS**.

Steve Jobs decided to make the power of movie-making accessible to the masses. By masses, he meant those having a MAC. By chance, I just bought a MAC and became a fan overnight. If I had a movie to show on my premier's night, it was thanks to Steve Jobs.

Then, a few years later, I decided to make Apple Computer my business partner. With iMacs, we got the dental space smarter and online. Until his departure from Apple and his death, I was at each of his keynotes. I remember once, as the doors of politics opened, I was telling myself that: "That's not real power, I want Steve Jobs' job or, even better, to be working with him! Not for him, but with him."

That being said, I followed his rise, disgrace and comeback to reach the moon and beyond. I was a passenger, and I learned all that I could. The insights of Alan Deutschman filled the voids I did not know about the life of Steve Jobs, giving me an even greater perspective of the Man, his Whys and the strength of his character.

It is said that a wise man will learn from his mistake. Well, in my last book, I had the chance to have Sharon Lechter as a special guest author, and she said it even with more clarity:

"If it is wise to learn from our mistakes, it is even wiser to learn from others' mistakes."
Sharon Lechter

This is what I got out for **THE SECOND COMING OF STEVE JOBS**, the genuine story of a man refusing to stand down, one convinced that it wasn't it; that he was meant for more. I followed his footstep and found my own **WAY TO ABUNDANCE**.

I will never have the chance to meet and to thank Steve Jobs in person, but from the words of those like Alan Deutschman and Walter Isaacson, I had the chance to walk into Steve Jobs' shoes, and thanks to **empathy**, I learned from his success and mistakes.

We each have our preferences and heroes. Here is one of mine, a man who showed me the possibilities, that twice, changed the course of my evolution with his inventions and boldness.

I can't resist to tell you a key moment I learn from the mistake of Steve Jobs as reported in **THE SECOND COMING OF STEVE JOBS**. In the late 80s, IBM was growing tired of **MS-DOS** and of Microsoft, Steve Jobs hated Bill Gates for stealing the **WINDOWS'** concept from the Mackintosh team.

Well, as Steve Jobs departed from **Apple**, he left with some key people to found **NeXT**. Steve is a hardware person, all he cares about the machine, not the software. That being said, the Operational System on which **NeXT** was running on caught the attention of **IBM**'s CEO.

IBM was unsuccessful in developing its own OS, so they turned to Steve Jobs as the alternative to Microsoft Windows. They had an agreement, but the day the lawyers of IBM went to Jobs with the contract, the contract was about an inch thick, well, Steve started to laugh and threw the contract in the garbage.

- Come back with a 5 pages contracts and I'll sign it.

The IBM people left, very perplexed. A few months went by and always nothing from IBM. Steve was not surfing on gold, NeXT and PIXAR were bleeding him dry. So he swallowed his pride and call IBM to know where they were with the contract.

Well, in the meantime, they changed CEO and the new administration decided to go with Microsoft instead. After that, Microsoft Windows became a household brand. Steve Jobs had the chance to beat Bill Gates right there, but he threw that in the garbage! Do you need a better lesson of humility? And those are only my words, wait to read the words of Alan, he is a true master, not just a reporter, but also a great storyteller.

And what about coming back? Well, Steve learned from that mistake. Almost a decade later, he used his OS to come back at Apple. Today's MAC OS X are all based on that OS licensed to Apple by Steve Jobs. And the rest is History!

You learned the **WHY**, the **WHAT**, the **HOW** and the **WHERE** in the first part of the **BOOTCAMP**. This is what is coming next on the journey, challenges and failures, and how to come back from them. For this reason, **THE SECOND COMING OF STEVE JOBS** is 5th on my list of the **BOOTCAMP**.

From **MILLION DOLLAR MINDSET,** this is **BOOTCAMP: 8 BOOKS TO REWRITE MINDSETS INTO WINNING STATES OF MIND.** Welcome to the **ALPHAS**.

Dr BAK NGUYEN

CHAPTER 6

BUSINESS @ THE SPEED OF THOUGHT
FROM BILL GATES AND COLLINS HEMINGWAY
by Dr BAK NGUYEN

William Henry Gates III, American business magnate, co-founder of Microsoft Corporation, investor, and philanthropist. Bill Gates is one of the best-known entrepreneurs and pioneers of the microcomputer revolution. He is now full-time invested in the Bill & Melinda Gates Foundation, the private charitable foundation that he and his wife, Melinda Gates, established in 2000. From 1995 to 2017, he held the Forbes title of the richest person in the world all but four of those years. In 2009, Gates and Warren Buffett founded The Giving Pledge, whereby they and other billionaires pledge to give at least half of their wealth to philanthropy.

AWARDED THE PRESIDENTIAL MEDAL OF FREEDOM 2016 - PADMA BHUSHAN 2015 - LASKER-BLOOMBERG PUBLIC SERVICE AWARD 2013 - BAMBI MILLENNIUM AWARD 2013 - SILVER BUFFALO AWARD 2010 - BOWER AWARD FOR BUSINESS LEADERSHIP 2010 - SATELLITE SPECIAL ACHIEVEMENT AWARD FOR OUTSTANDING CONTRIBUTION TO ENTERTAINMENT NEW MEDIA 1997 - DISTINGUISHED FELLOW OF THE BRITISH COMPUTER SOCIETY 1994 - NATIONAL MEDAL OF TECHNOLOGY AND INNOVATION 1992

Collins Hemingway, technologist and writer who has published five nonfiction books, including Bill Gates's #1 bestselling Business @ the Speed of Thought.

This one is a special one. 21 years after the facts, most of us will just say how evident business is at the age of the information highway. Everything is online with fast speed internet, LTE network and our smartphones, again, lead by Steve Jobs with the creation of the iPhone a little more than a decade ago.

Well, if today it seems to be a norm, 21 years ago, it was science fiction. We were still talking about TCP-IP as protocols for network and connection between computers.

Now, at the aftermath of the COVID war, all the resistant industries and the remnants of the past will either have to adapt to join the information revolution or they will all disappear... at high speed. If the technological shift started some 20 years ago, well, today it is do or die.

It started with the businesses, where each company, each store needed a virtual presence, looking for a **.com**. Then, that moved into the empowerment of each individual with the advent of **Facebook**, where each person was assigned a personal page.

In between, the new world order of **Google** mapped the entire ecosystem and **You Tube** replaced the media libraries, slowly but surely. The media push was accelerated and completed with the advent of **Netflix**.

On the air waves, **iTunes**, lead by Steve Jobs at **Apple**, started the digitalization and replacement of the radio frequencies. After the establishment of legal online music outlets, replacing the clandestine networks, **iTunes** grew to become the leader in music distribution, cutting the middleman out of the equation. Music streaming came next. Of course, many competitors joined in later on, **Spotify** to name one.

And what about talk shows? Well, that too got its channel, with the advent of PODCASTS. **Apple, Google, Spotify** all joined in. In the midst of the digitalization frenzy, a man with a dream to sell books online, 25 years ago, is now the richest man on the planet. Yes, I name Jeff Bezos, founder of **Amazon**. From books, he moves on to become the biggest world outlet.

For those businesses not upgraded to the 2.0 industries, **Shopify**, the world leader in e-commerce hosting surpassed the value of Canada biggest bank at the aftermath of the COVID war. What does that tell you? That the trend is real and accelerating.

What is next? Well, everything else! The health industry, the legal industry, the accounting industry, governments and even churches will all have to upgrade or be replaced. Well, 21 years ago, Bill Gates was describing all of this, a little like a prophet before the storm.

Bill Gates did more than predicting, he drove the narrative, he built the infrastructures and inspired the brainpower of the planet to join the Silicon Valley's vibe and ambition. The common theme coming with the technological wave is high speed and democratization. Nowadays, it is about right now and how to sort out the truth from the fake.

The printed Newspapers outlet disappeared, the Compact Disks and record stores too. Video renting morphed, from Blockbuster to Netflix. Cable company are struggling. Traditional books' publishing companies and the books outlets fight for their dignity, looking for an idea to escape fatality.

At the aftermath of the COVID war, the shopping centers too might be in danger, not able to compete with Amazon, Alibaba and Spotify. Office renting is now facing a new competitor: **ZOOM**. The virtual world describe in the Matrix more than 20 years ago is gaining speed and momentum.

If the technology itself wasn't appealing enough to push for adoption, well, the lawmakers, in the menace of the VIRUS of the 21st century, pushed the adoption, forcing the first worldwide shutdown of commercial activities.

Companies like **UBER** redefined the job market with democratization and, let's face it, lesser discrimination, allowing everyone an equal opportunity for labor, a position and the redefinition of their own schedule.

All of this is not in the book of Bill Gates, not in those precise words. But Bill paved the way to all of them, 21 years ago. And the title of his book is **BUSINESS @**

THE SPEED OF THOUGHT. It is proof of the power of the mind over the evolution of our civilization if you ask me.

BOOTCAMP is all about mindsets and states of mind. If you were not 100% convinced that you mindsets and states of mind could rewrite your destiny and the world's, well, Bill Gates and Steve Jobs proved otherwise. And they did it with vision, with words and, eventually, with money, a lot of money.

I missed most of Bill Gates prophecies, 18 years ago, as I listened to his audiobook on my way to Hollywood, driving down the US 1 from San Francisco to Los Angeles. I was fascinated by the vision, but being a dentist looking to follow his dream in movie making, I missed the opportunities and the readings of the future. I could have surfed the dawn of the digitalization of movie-making, I was amongst its pioneers.

Instead, I came back to Montreal and conformed myself to fit in the ranks of the health industry, playing it safe and being heavily regulated. I rose up, 20 years later, as a leader, an Alpha, but not a titan. History will tell what the Alpha will become.

18 years ago, I choose my licence to practice and my family over my own thoughts and ambitions. And with it, I lost most of my speed and my powers. For the last three years, you listened to me talking about speed, teaching you how to build momentum. Well, all of that, I learned some 18 years prior with the vision of Bill Gates and the words of Collins Hemingway.

All of this was 21 years ago, why is it still relevant? Well, because take away the words and the examples, even the prophecies, and what is left is what I understood 18 years ago: **THE SPEED OF THOUGHT**.

Even if Bill Gates's book, **BUSINESS @ THE SPEED OF THOUGHT** is in the second part of this book, well it is not just an example, but a true recipe for success, one within his title.

I strongly recommend everyone to read this book very carefully and to see what was written 21 years ago. Read and take the time to visualize how long each statement took to materialized. Where were you and what were you doing missing out on the opportunity? Yes, that we each missed!

By now, in your **BOOTCAMP**, you have already awakened your mind and your senses. It is time to face the mirror, the test of self-evaluation to identify the flaws and the needed improvements. Writing this chapter did just that for me.

I've missed the revolution as I was standing right at its doorsteps, driving between Silicon Valley and Hollywood. I had the mind and saw the vision, but I chose my legacy as a doctor instead. 18 years later, it is still time for me to right those bad decisions and to leverage my regrets.

I changed industry, from Entertainment and Movie-Making into Education and Health. Well, 2 years ago, I received the title of Industries' Disruptor. 3 years ago, I discovered a talent for words, written and spoken. And now, in the midst of the COVID war, I see the crying needs of upgrades of both the health and education industries. This is my awakening, the titan is coming. **Mdex V** and **Mdex 7** are coming. Watch me.

And this is why **BUSINESS @ THE SPEED OF THOUGHT** written by Bill Gates and Collins Hemingway is next on the list of the **BOOTCAMP**, one to confront you to the **MIRROR OF YOUR DESTINY**.

From **MILLION DOLLAR MINDSET,** this is **BOOTCAMP: 8 BOOKS TO REWRITE MINDSETS INTO WINNING STATES OF MIND.** Welcome to the **ALPHAS**.

Dr BAK NGUYEN

CHAPTER 7
DELIVERING HAPPINESS
FROM TONY HSIEH
by Dr BAK NGUYEN

Tony Hsieh, American Internet entrepreneur and venture capitalist, CEO of the online shoes and clothing company Zappos. Prior to joining Zappos, Tony Hsieh co-founded the Internet advertising network LinkExchange, which he sold to Microsoft in 1998 for $265 million. In 2009, Zappos was sold to Amazon in a deal valued at approximately $1.2 billion.

AWARDED ERNST & YOUNG ENTREPRENEUR OF THE YEAR AWARD FOR THE NORTHERN CALIFORNIA REGION IN 2007 - WORLD CHAMPIONS - ACM INTERNATIONAL COLLEGIATE PROGRAMMING CONTEST - HARVARD UNIVERSITY TEAM 1993

I took the habit to have the height of my crescendos and emotional rise at the 2/3 of each of my books, and that since day one with, **SYMPHONY OF SKILLS**. If I keep writing, it is a little in the *encore mentality* of the artists and performers: one more song, one more applause, one more cheer.

Well, I've been on stage and on camera. What I love most is the before and after. It is there when you feel like an insider, someone with real access, before and after the spotlights. This is me alone with you, after the spotlights and the applauses.

After Steve Jobs and Bill Gates, after the **MIRROR OF DESTINY**, what's next? Well, a rest. A pause to let the information sink in and to give ourselves a chance to digest the transformation ignited inside.

A little like Steve Jobs and his infamous: "Oh, one last thing…" Well, here is mine. Building for the future, can we do it with fun too? Tony Hsieh, founder of **Zappos** gave me that hope in his book, **DELIVERING HAPPINESS**.

Tony is an e-Entrepreneur who made it, not just once but twice! He found and sold two of his endeavours: **LinkExchange** and **Zappos**, and he has such a different narrative than the Silicon Valley's Millionaires. After the millions he received from the sale of **LinkExchange**, Tony had experience and recognition, he was looking for fun and excitement.

DELIVERING HAPPINESS narrated his path and journey as he left the company he founded to sell shoes! Literally, selling shoes. But the second time, most of his attention was focus on the customer experience, the team building experience and the work environment. His executives often referred to his new ideas as the **Tony's social experiments**.

Well, a few years later and 1.2 Billion later, his vision of social Experiments was one of a kind. This is no coming back or to make it yet again, this is the evolution in the journey, to seek for the **POWER OF HAPPINESS**, of delivering happiness.

After my regrets turning my back on Hollywood and evolving at the speed of regulation instead of the pace of my thoughts, I found comfort in Tony's words.

I was a dentist wearing a white coat and delivering happiness on a daily basis, one smile after the next.

I was already ahead of the curve, since my peers were delivering health, one tooth at a time. I was at least seeing the person in his or her as wholeness, one soul to another.

I told you many times by now that if I made it in dentistry, it was because my patients saved me. As I was thirsty for human connection, my patients were all too happy to connect to avoid the discussion of pain and teeth. Until I had to operate… but their trust, I got first.

That made me into a rising star in a profession I despite. Today, I do not know what else I could do, I've been a dentist, a loved one, for the last 20 years. I am an entrepreneur and I have the track record to prove my resilience and creativity… until I faced the **MIRROR OF DESTINY**.

I built **Mdex & Co**, the corporation with which I am leading the dental industry to the **INFORMATION AGE** and speeding its advent to the **COLLABORATION AGE**. I got the attention and the favor of the financial world since my launch because I understood the ratios and the narrative.

In the COVID war, I rose in influence as an **ALPHA** player and a thought leader of my industry on a global scale. I have the chance to be surrounded by mentors, all titans and leaders in their field, **medicine**, **technology** and **finance**. I got their interests because me too, I was interested in a social experiment, one to make the world a better place.

I met with Jean De Serres, former CEO of **Hema Quebec**, the equivalent of the RED CROSS in my province, as I was trying to establish a new network to serve the cause of the stem cells.

That one failed, but we were so close and making progress in weeks as the norms were measured in years. If our friendship sealed around our love for music, well, I gained his respect because I was trying to help and almost succeeded. To him, the failure was never mine.

I kept and still keep the interest of Christian Trudeau, former founder and president of **BCE Emergis**, because I am bold and articulated. Christian built 18 billion in value, at the top of the stock market, for the number one telecom giant in Canada.

I gained his affection and friendship as he truly understood my profound wish to make life better, not only for my patients but also for my peers, especially, the younger generations.

Today, I am his biggest bet, one of *changing the world from a dental chair*. Once again, it was a social experiment. I even had the Federal government of Canada backing me up for a long term study in the happiness' index of health professionals... that project is still trying to find footing within the scientific community.

I met with Andre Chatelain, former first vice-president of the **MOUVEMENT DESJARDINS**, the biggest french banking cooperative in North America. He was managing 100 billion in volume transactions, leading the credit and VISA divisions. Well, we became friends too, as he was intrigued by my energy and boldness to reform an industry, the most conservative dental and health industry.

He likes my vision and narrative, but what he loved was the genuine passion committing to build sustainable infrastructures with a human touch. On that, he joined Christian, they both decided to back me the day they saw my ways with my under links and the people under my influence.

His presence has brought **Mdex** to the next level with, not a corporate culture, but taking my warmth from the customer service to the human resource department, making **Mdex & Co**, a first of its kind.

Under the leadership of Tranie Vo, co-founder of **Mdex & Co**, my wife and COO, we navigated the COVID war with much challenges and rising as an industry leader thanks to the involvement of our team, **TEAM Mdex**.

Throughout the year, **TEAM Mdex** changed more than once, sometime up to 90% within a very short period. Those were dark days. The leadership did not changed, it grew instead. The body changed and even revolted, leaving massively. What held **Mdex** together was its clientele, its patients. The presence of Andre mentoring Tranie allowed the transfer of that success to Human Resources.

Now, we are ready for national expansion and the spine of the world future of dentistry and health telecommunication is waiting to be written with our thoughts. Once again, a social experiment.

I only read **DELIVERING HAPPINESS** once, but that concept of human evolution and of connecting genuinely stuck with me. Taking on the **BOOTCAMP**, we all have different ideas, different hopes, different dreams. We were also all confronted with the same demons:

"More than just to be or not to be, but to leave what we know and what we currently are behind for a hope, not even a promise, that's entrepreneurship."
Dr Bak Nguyen

Whatever your age, how do you deal with such a dilemma, betting your life and future on a hope? Well,

Tony Hsieh brought you the answer, one served on a silver platter: **HAPPINESS**.

Seeking your own happiness, you might have look elsewhere, but building social experiments in order to deliver happiness and improving it, on a daily basis, is a sure recipe for success and to change the world for the better.

Super rockstar, Sting, sang that to change the world, one must first change one's mind. Well, who amongst us do not seek happiness? Changing the world and building the next big thing might not be that far away after all!

Still not convinced yet? How does one come back from turning his back on Hollywood? By being a dentist? I wish that was true. I survived and grew back to the **table of Influence** because I never ceased looking and **deliver Happiness**.

I changed industry. What I miss in 2002, at the dawn of the digitalization of the movie industry, I studied and learned from the masters of the tech revolution to be ready. Now, 18 years later in an other industry, one much larger in importance and capitalization: the health industry, it is my time to rise. From there, the extension to the education industry is one step away.

History will tell if I have made it or not, but if you keep hearing about my work and my name, it will be because I kept pushing for better ways to deliver happiness to more and more people. Some sell shoes, I sell genuine connections. We agreed on the selling part and on the happiness part, what we were selling was just an excuse to connect with each of you.

Even if you have graduated from the **BOOTCAMP, DELIVERING HAPPINESS** written by Tony Hsieh is next on the list of the **BOOTCAMP**. The fun has just begun!

"Look for happiness, share happiness, deliver happiness. Success is the next stop."
Dr Bak Nguyen

From **MILLION DOLLAR MINDSET,** this is **BOOTCAMP: 8 BOOKS TO REWRITE MINDSETS INTO WINNING STATES OF MIND.** Welcome to the **ALPHAS**.

Dr BAK NGUYEN

CHAPTER 8

WIKINOMICS:
HOW MASS COLLABORATION CHANGES
EVERYTHING FROM DON TAPSCOTT AND ANTHONY
D. WILLIAMS

by Dr BAK NGUYEN

Don Tapscott, Canadian business executive, author, consultant and speaker. CEO of the Tapscott Group and the co-founder and Executive Chairman of the Blockchain Research Institute. He is the former Chancellor of his alma mater Trent University, and is currently an Adjunct Professor of Technology and Operations Management at INSEAD. Authored or co-authored 16 books on the application of technology in business and society. His 2006 book, Wikinomics: How Mass Collaboration Changes Everything (2006), co-authored by Anthony D. Williams, was an international bestseller, was number one on the 2007 management book charts and has been translated into 20 different languages.

AWARDED DOCTOR OF LAWS (HONORIS CAUSA) — GRANTED BY THE UNIVERSITY OF ALBERTA IN 2001, TRENT UNIVERSITY IN 2006, AND MCMASTER UNIVERSITY IN 2010. MEMBER OF THE ORDER OF CANADA IN 2015.

Anthony D. Williams, consultant, researcher, and author; vice president of research with international think tank New Paradigm. Williams is also the CEO and Co-Founder of Canadian think-tank, The DEEP Centre. His work has been featured in publications including Business Week and The Globe and Mail and the Times of India.

What a journey! This is day 5 of writing and the last chapter of this book. After this one, the conclusion and boom! I will be done with my 71st book! After the hope of building with happiness, for happiness, how can we still add on to such a majestic journey?

How about showing you the big picture? That picture, I got only two decades later. If Paulo showed me the perspective of the myriad of journeys; if Robert and Sharon gave me the key to investment and finance; if Darren gave me a sure recipe for success; I learned from Steve and Bill that writing the future is possible with my words and vision, but it would take 20 years after my initial awakening for me to discover how it all comes together.

Wikinomics, written by Don Tapscott and Anthony D. Williams was a fortunate read. I was just wandering at **INDIGO**, a Sunday evening looking for inspiration. Tranie and I have that habit to go out looking for inspiration on Sunday evenings. She likes walking and the coffee at Starbuck, I like wandering within knowledge and possibilities: **INDIGO** book outlet was the perfect place for both of us.

Within one of those evenings, I stumble upon that title, **WIKINOMICS**. That was a new audiobook that I never saw before. I picked it up and read the synopsis in the back. Interesting! I was looking for something to read anyway... we had a road trip planned soon. I can't remember where to.

I opened the box on the road and put the first CD in. Then, the second. And third... I went through **WIKINOMICS** just like watching a very interesting documentary on National Geographic. Without summarizing the book, I can tell you how interesting the narrative was. They proposed to link delink all of the dots and to relink the causal-effect differently. These new links then, tell us a different story of social evolution.

WIKINOMICS is about linking the dots, those dots stuck in different and unrelated narratives. Here is my favorite passage:

In the late 80s, crime was through the roof in the USA. It is around that time that ROBOCOP came to the screen, with the idea of protecting cities crippled by crimes. If the current stage would continue, the crime syndicate would have representatives on National polling with their growing numbers.

Republicans and Democrats leaderships invested billions of dollar in the law enforcement in prevision of the climbing crime rate curve projected. The scenario was catastrophic!

And then, on the national average, the curve dropped drastically all across the country. Not flattened, dropped, like an airplane going down and crashing. The politicians were very proud and saluted their efforts… but the billions invested was still in the preparation phase… What could explain such steep decline of the crime rate?

Well, two decades earlier, abortion was legalized in the USA. Very hard to hear and even harder to say, all those unwanted children who were never born, contributed to the steep decline of the crime rate. What seems unrelated a minute ago just change completely the narrative and the perspective of how society and its values are impacting the future.

Not everyone agreed with the causal effect association of Don Tapscott and Anthony D. Williams, but they proved a much more important point: we should question and challenge the narrative and look for more way to understand the story.

That broke what was left in me from my formal and strict education. I told you how a free thinker and a bold driver I can be, solving a crisis in the health industry with the glam of the movie industry once, and then, looking at dentists to reinforce the stem cells network, it was me applying the idea of making different associations, delinking and rebounding the dots differently.

Sometimes it leads to nowhere. Other times, an interesting idea will come out of the mix. And those new ideas aren't perfect nor the best solution, but if you keep pushing three phases down the road, reapplying the same method of delinking and rebounding differently, well, you just created something new.

*"Hammering air three times over
and it will become steel."*
Dr Bak Nguyen

You've created something new and familiar at the same time since the pieces you are utilizing are from everyday life. That put you way ahead in practicability since your resources are within reach and often, abundant. You just provide a new blueprint to link the dots together.

Now, WILL is what you will need to materialize such ideas. The will to do things differently. This is where the real challenge comes. People just do not like to change their habits and they are too lazy to delink to rebond. This is a sad reality for you to accept, until a crisis hit and the quest for a solution is much needed.

"For as long as the pain is greater than the pain of change, you have a chance to proceed."
Dr Bak Nguyen

There are so many other examples, cool examples in **WIKINOMICS**, but those will be for you to read and to reflect on. The point here was not to draw conclusions upon a crazy idea and to revolutionize the world, but to stretch your mind accepting the possibility of different scenarios, different narratives and different possibilities.

Life is dynamic and everything has a ripple effect affecting all around it. Each ripple effect adds on. Some will just cause a wave and fade. Some with sum up and some will compound its effect to a much larger scale. Be open to see, be open to feel and then, be flexible to readjust.

"Forget good and bad, the world is not linear.
Look for cause and effect, those are
from the ripple effects."
Dr Bak Nguyen

What started as a simple read open my mind to a world of possibilities and different perspective. As a surgeon, I was trained to have a laser sight with laser focus. My training with different mentors from different fields showed me how I could apply such training to different problems, in some many different fields.

By the end of the day, everything is about problem-solving. Well, **WIKINOMICS** remove the screws keeping my head and vision still. Now, I can scan the world with a laser focus sight and ask questions and seek for new creative solutions recycling the elements on the board.

If you were looking to understand what creativity is, this is a great introduction and a must-do exercise! For this reason, **WIKINOMICS**, written by Don Tapscott and Anthony D. Williams closes the **BOOTCAMP** as the 8th book.

Accept that the world can be different,
And you life will change.
Accept that we do not see and know everything,
And you've unburdened yourself
From Pride and the lies of Perfection.
Accept to adapt with flexibility of mind and skills,
And you will evolve.

From **MILLION DOLLAR MINDSET,** this is **BOOTCAMP: 8 BOOKS TO REWRITE MINDSETS INTO WINNING STATES OF MIND.** Welcome to the **ALPHAS**.

Dr BAK NGUYEN

CONCLUSION

by Dr BAK NGUYEN

Wow, what a beautiful journey. If you have waited to finish this book to start with your first read, well, stop reading and start with **THE ALCHEMIST** right away! Then, as you finish THE ALCHEMIST, come back and read the second chapter before going to the next book, **RICH DAD POOR DAD**.

And so on, by week 3, you'll be on **THE COMPOUND EFFECT** and then, move on to **THIS IS YOUR TIME**. By the end of part I of your **BOOTCAMP**, I advise you to take a few days break, one week at the most, to vent the accumulation of new knowledge.

Then, as you will be applying these new perspectives to your life and work, read in parallel the books of part II, **THE SECOND COMING OF STEVE JOBS**, **BUSINESS @ THE SPEED OF THOUGHT** and **DELIVERING HAPPINESS**. Read those as you are incrementing changes into your life. Doing so, you ensure that the changes have started. You will also have the impression to evolve by the side of Steve Jobs, Bill Gates and Tony Hsieh. Imagine to have these minds as classmates!

Then as finished the 7th book, I will advise you to write a chapter of your own, even if you are not a writer. Nobody but you, has to read your writing. At this point, write about your journey, what you have, not learned, but experienced.

This is a **BOOTCAMP**, not a classroom. That chapter of yours will confirm that you have successfully graduated from the **BOOTCAMP** to rewrite your mindsets into winning states of mind. Writing as that state of mind.

And then, only then, you can move forward to read the 8th book, **WIKINOMICS** to see how much further you can extend your powers and reach. Each time, go back and forth to this book to keep proximity with me. I will serve as your coach for the next 2 months.

This is the blueprint and the program of **BOOTCAMP**. So why now? Why are you reading about this only in the conclusion? Because doing so you will be reading this book twice! Just kidding.

Seriously, it is because we needed to rewrite our mindset first. Most of us are hardwired to learn first and to implement later. Most of us will also love to enjoy a ride as a passenger to be inspired and to benefit from the "**FREERIDE**". That's okay, I am been trained that way too!

Now that the **FREERIDE** is over, you are ready to embrace your destiny with action. The action is not only to read the next book but to extract its essence and to compare your experience with mine. Look in the mirror and have that discussion with yourself, thinking that you are exchanging with me. Tell me about your journey.

Then, from one book to the next, you are meeting your mentors, one by one. Each one will be introducing you to the power of the universe within your mind. Read and have something to write about. In other words, read for inspiration and guidance and come back to the mirror with stories of your own. This is about actions and changes, not about watching others succeed.

Writing these words, I wished I had such support and guidance when I was looking for myself. I envy you, each of you. I envy the excitement and the joy as you will discover your powers and the possibilities laying ahead. Sure, I have mine too, but the feeling is a great one and one of such intensity, especially the first time. Envoy your rise, enjoy your journey, enjoy your new-found powers.

A word of advice before I let you go to your destiny. Remember that to learn and to grow, you must be open and available. Let go of the past and of what you know. If that was enough, you won't be reading this book. Medals and pains, leave all of those behind to free the space both your heart and your mind to welcome fresh air, fresh perspectives, fresh hopes.

The growth is consequential, not from the accumulation of knowledge, but by the passage of wisdom and experience coming through the channel, you! Feel and live the experience and let go, have fun!

"Evolution is not about accumulating but about experiencing."
Dr Bak Nguyen

So be open to grow. To grow even more, be generous and grateful. The more you give, the more the size of your heart grow to welcome even more information and perspectives.

And just like the **BOOTCAMP** has changed you into a new person, keep that habit to reinvent yourself daily. You have the knowledge, you have the flexibility, you just need to keep the desire fire up.

By the end of the day, we are all doing this to seek happiness. Well, staying still and secure will not bring happiness, on the contrary, those bears boredom in their hearts. Do you know how to leverage boredom to evolve? Or is boredom be the virus that will undo most of your evolution?

The best way to fight boredom is to prevent its advent. Reinvent yourself with fun and a touch of humor. Take your duty seriously, never yourself. And, by the end of each day, face your **MIRROR OF DESTINY** and report what you've done within that day.

If you hate your day, well, flush it and start fresh tomorrow. If you loved it, well, flush it too and start fresh again tomorrow! And while you are at it, try beating your own score! This is how your momentum and legend will rise.

Be open, be good, be great for the future of our kind. Lead the way to **ABUNDANCE**, **PEACE** and **HAPPINESS,** those are the powers you have inherited.

Now, the fate of tomorrow is in your hands. My brothers and sisters in arms, I salute you.

From **MILLION DOLLAR MINDSET,** this is **BOOTCAMP: 8 BOOKS TO REWRITE MINDSETS INTO WINNING STATES OF MIND.** Welcome to the **ALPHAS**.

Dr BAK NGUYEN

ABOUT THE AUTHOR

From Canada, **Dr BAK NGUYEN**, Nominee EY Entrepreneur of the year, Grand Homage LYS DIVERSITY, and LinkedIn & TownHall Achiever of the year. Dr Bak is a cosmetic dentist, CEO and founder of Mdex & Co. His company is revolutionizing the dental field. Speaker and motivator, he wrote more than 70 books in 35 months accumulating many world records (to be officialized). He is on the quest to set the next word record of writing 72 books / 36 months. His books are covering:

- **ENTREPRENEURSHIP**
- **LEADERSHIP**
- **QUEST OF IDENTITY**
- **DENTISTRY AND MEDICINE**
- **PARENTING**
- **CHILDREN BOOKS**
- **PHILOSOPHY**

In 2003, he founded Mdex, a dental company upon which in 2018, he launched the most ambitious private endeavour to reform the dental industry, Canada wide. Philosopher, he has close to his heart the quest of happiness of the people surrounding him, patients and colleagues alike. In 2020, he launched an International collaborative initiative named **THE ALPHAS** to share knowledge and to Entrepreneurs and Doctors to thrive through the Greatest Pandemic and Economic depression of our time.

These projects have allowed Dr Nguyen to attract interests from the international and diplomatic community and he is now the center of a global discussion in the wellbeing and the future of the health profession. It is in that matter that he shares his thoughts and encourages the health community to share their own stories.

"It's not worth it go through it alone! Together, we stand, alone, we fall."

Motivational speaker and serial entrepreneur, philosopher and author, from his own words, Dr Nguyen describes himself as a dentist by circumstances, an entrepreneur by nature and a communicator by passion. He also holds recognitions from the Canadian Parliament and the Canadian Senate.

www.DrBakNguyen.com

AMAZON - APPLE BOOKS - KINDLE - SPOTIFY - APPLE MUSIC

UAX

ULTIMATE AUDIO EXPERIENCE

A new way to learn and enjoy Audiobooks. Made to be entertaining while keeping the self-educational value of a book, UAX will appeal to both auditive and visual people. UAX is the blockbuster of the Audiobooks.

UAX will cover most of Dr Bak's books, and is now negotiating to bring more authors and more titles to the UAX concept. Now streaming on Spotify, Apple Music and available for download on all major music platforms. Give it a try today!

www.DrBakNguyen.com

FROM THE SAME AUTHOR
Dr Bak Nguyen

www.DrBakNguyen.com

132

133

www.DrBakNguyen.com

AMAZON · APPLE BOOKS · KINDLE · SPOTIFY · APPLE MUSIC

DR.

Bak Nguyen

www.DrBakNguyen.com

www.ingramcontent.com/pod-product-compliance
Lightning Source LLC
Chambersburg PA
CBHW062023200326
41519CB00017B/4901